Know Your Trucks

Patrick W Dyer

Old Pond Publishing

First published 2009

ISBN 978-1-906853-19-8

Published by
Old Pond Publishing Ltd
Dencora Business Centre
36 White House Road
Ipswich IP1 5LT
United Kingdom

www.oldpond.com

Cover photograph: DAF LF55 4 x 2 rigid with drawbar trailer and de-mountable box bodies

Book design by Liz Whatling
Printed and bound in China

Contents

For more information see 'International classifying system', 'Truck Talk' and 'Anatomy of a truck' at the end of the book.

Acknowledgements

My thanks to the following: Tony Pain, John Comer, Nigel Hanwell, Lisa Fuller, Simon Wood, Penny Randall, Les Bishop, Joe Baker, Simon Eggleton, Keith Child, John Swain, David Booty, Richard Calder, Sue Chapman, Liz Madden and John Wood Henderson.

Author's **N**ote

Manufacturers' names and models are included for identification purposes only.
All figures relating to vehicle spec are taken from the manufacturer's own literature and can be subject to change. The author cannot be held responsible for any errors.

Picture **C**redits

Plate *(1)* Isuzu Truck UK Ltd, *(2)* Volvo Group UK Ltd, *(3)* John W Henderson, *(5)* Mercedes-Benz UK Ltd, *(6)* Isuzu Truck UK Ltd, *(7)* Plasmoor Concrete Products, *(8)* Isuzu Truck UK Ltd, *(9)* Iveco Ltd, *(10)* Mercedes-Benz UK Ltd, *(11)* DAF Trucks Ltd, *(12)* ES Group Ltd, *(13)* & *(14)* DAF Trucks Ltd, *(15)* Isuzu Truck UK Ltd, *(17)* Mercedes-Benz UK Ltd, *(18)* Iveco Ltd, *(19)* DAF Trucks Ltd, *(20)* John W Henderson, *(21)* Mercedes-Benz UK Ltd, *(22)* & *(23)* DAF Trucks Ltd, *(24)* Mercedes-Benz UK Ltd, *(25)* DAF Trucks Ltd, *(26)* Mercedes-Benz UK Ltd, *(28)* DAF Trucks Ltd, *(29)* Iveco Ltd, *(30)* & *(31)* Volvo Group UK Ltd, *(32)*, *(33)* & *(34)* Mercedes-Benz UK Ltd, *(35)* DAF Trucks Ltd, *(36)* Iveco Ltd, *(37)* DAF Trucks Ltd, *(39)* Volvo Group UK Ltd, *(40)* Mercedes-Benz UK Ltd, *(41)*, *(42)* & *(43)* Volvo Group UK Ltd, *(44)* Iveco Ltd, *(Cutaway 'Anatomy of a Truck')* Volvo Group UK Ltd.

Foreword

Trucks (or lorries) are all around us. Virtually everything that we eat, drink, wear, ride, drive and, in many cases, live in has at some time been delivered by a truck.

Trucks form the backbone of industry, feeding the factories with the raw materials and components which enable them to create the end products that are then collected by trucks to be delivered to the shops, dealers and end users. The world economy is dependent on trucks to keep the goods moving, allowing trade between countries to flourish.

With its origins in the early part of the last century, the truck has developed over the years into a highly specialised tool with a staggering

range of variants to fulfil a multitude of tasks. Stringent regulations ensure that trucks are now some of the most efficient and cleanest vehicles on the road.

As a book of this size could not adequately cover the variants of just one model range from just one manufacturer, we decided it would be better to explain to you the purpose of some of the more common types of trucks that you will see every day on our roads.

PATRICK W DYER
2009

Description

Flatbed Rigid

At a glance

Flat load platform,
two to four axles

Use

General cargo sometimes
covered with a tarpaulin

The flatbed truck once formed the backbone of
the UK's haulage fleets. It is a versatile vehicle
capable of carrying any load within the vehicle's
weight category as long as it will fit within the
confines of the bed. The vertical panel behind the
cab is known as the headboard and its purpose is
to stop the load moving forward.

This example is mounted on a Japanese Isuzu
N75.190 4 x 2 chassis. The engine, a 4-cylinder
diesel, is turbocharged and intercooled, developing
190 hp.

2.

Description

Flatbed Rigid (self-loading)

At a glance

Flat load platform. Two to four axles. Hydraulic crane behind cab or at rear of chassis

Use

Delivery of large static loads

The ability for a truck to self-load is highly desirable and in some cases a necessity. Mobile site offices, for instance, cannot be unloaded by hand and are often delivered to a building site before any other plant so the vehicle delivering them must also be able to unload itself.

This Volvo FE is a 6 x 2 chassis with a rear steer tag axle which greatly improves its manoeuvrability over a non-steered type. The driver can control the hydraulic arm from a remote unit.

Description

Flatbed Artic

At a glance
Flat load platform. Two or three axles on tractor unit. One to three axles on trailer

Use
General cargo. Loads sometimes covered with a tarpaulin

When used in articulated form the flatbed is capable of carrying large amounts of goods, in this case up to 25 tonnes of wood products. Loads must be secured with ropes, straps or chains and, if required, might also be covered with tailored tarpaulins, a practice known as roping and sheeting.

This 38-tonne GVW combination is hauled by an ERF EC series, 4 x 2 tractor with a 10-litre Cummins engine. The EC range was the last produced by this famous English company before it was taken over by MAN of Germany in 2000.

Specialised Flatbed

At a glance
Flat load platform. Two or three axle tractor unit. One to three axle trailer

Use
Adapted to individual purpose

Description

Almost all types of trailer can be adapted to suit the special requirements of operators. This tri-axle flatbed, manufactured by the Dutch company, Broshuis, has a special bogie with three sets of steerable wheels to allow access to awkward sites such as railway stations and depots. It is also extendable to allow the carriage of 27-metre track sections.

This Mercedes-Benz Actros carries its own crane, which has a 10-tonne lifting capacity for unloading. The 6 x 4 chassis aids traction in difficult off-road conditions.

Description

Beaver-tailed Flat

At a glance
Flat load platform with downward angled section behind the rearmost wheels

Use
Plant and vehicle transport

The beaver-tailed flat allows a standard-height load platform to be loaded with vehicles or plant which can be driven up onto it. The drop section at the rear of the platform, the beaver tail, forms a continuous slope with the loading ramps to gain access. This type is less suitable for loading tall vehicles because the increased centre of gravity would make handling unsafe.

This Mercedes-Benz Actros 2536 6 x 2 is fitted with an Adblue diesel additive system, the tank for which is mounted behind the front wheel.

Description

Drop-side Rigid

At a glance
Flat load platform with large hinged panels around the edge. Two to four axles

Use
Typically sheet and tube metal, metal fabrications, building supplies and scaffolding

The drop-side body is a development of the flatbed that uses hinged panels which flap down against the chassis to assist loading and unloading. When in the raised position the panels lock on over-centre catches to provide restraint for the load. The drop-side is popular within the building supply trade.

The ISUZU 11-tonne chassis uses a 5.2-litre, 4-cylinder diesel engine giving 210 hp and a 6-speed manual gearbox. ISUZU also offer a 9-speed unit and an automatic option.

Description

Brick and Block Drawbar (self-loading)

At a glance
Flat or drop-sided load platform. Two or three axles on truck. Two or three axles on trailer. Hydraulic crane mounted behind cab or at rear of chassis

Use
Building material supply

The flatbed drawbar combination can offer operational advantages over the same weight articulated truck, particularly on work such as building material supply. The tri-axle trailer here is referred to as a centre-axle type, the bogie being inboard of the trailer ends. The loading crane, mounted at the rear of the truck chassis, has ample reach to unload both the front of the truck and the rear of the trailer.

Hino's 700 series covers the 18- to 44-tonne sectors. This 2838 example has a 6 x 2 chassis and is fitted with Hino's 13-litre engine, giving 380 hp.

Box Van Rigid

At a glance
Permanent box body covering load area. Rear doors or roller shutter. Two to four axles

Use
General cargo. Often multi-drop loads

Description

The box van was developed to protect and contain the load. Construction from ribbed or sandwiched aluminium offers strength without the penalty of high weight. Inside there are often channels in the floor and sides with eyelets for securing the load with straps.

This example is mounted on a 12-tonne ISUZU chassis with a 7.8-litre engine. The truck is fitted with an aerodynamic aid (often called a deflector) on the cab roof to smooth airflow over the front of the box to improve fuel economy.

Box Van Drawbar

At a glance

Permanently enclosed load areas. Rear and/or side doors. Two or three axles on truck. Two or three axles on trailer

Use

General cargo, specifically bulky items such as furniture

Description

The drawbar can offer advantages over the articulated trailer, particularly if the operator's loads tend to be 'high cube' where volume is greater than weight. Multi-drop loads can be split, allowing the trailer to be parked up once empty and collected later, saving on operating costs and improving access to some deliveries.

The IVECO Stralis 4 x 2 featured is fitted with the IVECO Cursor 10-litre engine, giving 450 hp and an Active Time (AT) high roof sleeper-cab, offering high levels of comfort and storage for the driver.

Description

Box Van Traditional Drawbar

At a glance
Permanently enclosed load areas. Rear and/or side doors. Two to three axles on truck. Two to three axles on trailer

Use
General cargo. Medium to long distance

The traditional drawbar differs from the centre-axle type with the trailer being fitted with one axle at the front and one or two at the back. The front axle is connected to a turntable and A-frame which allows it to steer. The system may be heavier than the centre-axle alternative, but stability is better and tyre scrub when manoeuvring is greatly reduced.

This Mercedes-Benz Atego 1529 has a 15-tonne GVW capacity as a solo rigid and is fitted with a 290 hp engine.

Description

Box Van Artic

At a glance

Permanently enclosed load area. Rear and/or side doors. Two to three axle tractor unit. One to three axle trailer

Use

General cargo, often palletised

Box van trailers can be dropped off to be loaded or unloaded as required and then swapped to repeat the process. In big depots trucks known as shunters will move trailers around for this purpose 24 hours a day, while road-going tractor units deliver them to their destinations.

The DAF XF105 is a further development of the XF95 which was introduced in 1997. It features parent company PACCAR's 12.9-litre MX engine. This example is a 6 x 2 with a mid-lift axle which can be raised when running empty or light.

Description

Step-frame Box Van Artic

At a glance

Permanently enclosed load area. Rear and/or side doors. Drop-in trailer chassis behind tractor unit. Two to three axle tractor. One to three axle trailer

Use

General cargo, furniture, hanging garments and sound equipment

Another way of gaining space for loads that 'cube out' is the step-frame trailer. With these types, the trailer chassis drops down behind the tractor unit, gaining depth and volume. This tri-axle example is operated by a company that specialises in concert tours and exhibition work, with loads that are very bulky but relatively light.

The DAF XF 95 was the first new product to emerge from DAF following the takeover by the American PACCAR Company in 1997. It was simple and robustly engineered, endearing it to drivers and operators alike.

Description

Refrigerated Rigid

At a glance
Permanently enclosed load area. Rear and/or side doors. Refrigeration unit mounted on front bulkhead or on chassis. Two to four axles

Use
Chilled and frozen goods, fresh produce

It was the advances in frozen food technologies in the 1960s that brought rise to the refrigerated truck which is now one of the most numerous types on our roads. This type of small rigid is often to be found supplying pubs, restaurants and smaller shops throughout the UK with chilled goods.

The DAF LF45 range covers the 7.5- to 21-tonne sectors with two engines from the PACCAR stable. The 4.5-litre, 4-cylinder FR develops between 140 and 185 hp, while the 6.7-litre, 6-cylinder GR develops 220 to 285 hp.

Description

Refrigerated Artic

At a glance

Permanently enclosed load area. Rear and/or side doors. Refrigeration unit mounted on front bulkhead or chassis of trailer. Two to three axle tractor unit. One to three axle trailer

Use

Long-distance bulk delivery of chilled, frozen and fresh produce, usually palletised

Generally, the refrigerator motor is mounted on the front bulkhead of the trailer. However, there are circumstances where this is not possible or desirable, and then it is often placed underneath the trailer chassis. This twin axle example is very typical of the type operated by supermarket chains.

The DAF CF85 in basic trim makes an ideal fleet tractor and has found favour with many operators with constant turn-around schedules. This example has the entry level 410 hp engine and standard, low roof sleeper cab.

Curtainsider Rigid

At a glance
Load area permanently enclosed front, top and back. Retractable curtain sides. Often fitted with rear doors. Two to four axles

Use
General cargo, often palletised

Description

The curtainsider has come to prominence in UK haulage, overtaking the flatbed as the format of choice for many operating in general haulage. While still offering good weather protection and load security, the curtainsider scores over the box van in the total access to the load area afforded by the curtains. This allows large items to be loaded through the sides and makes multi-drop loads easier to access.

The ISUZU rigid in this photo is a 4 x 2 F180-260, illustrating that it is an 18-tonne chassis fitted with a 260 hp engine.

Curtainsider Drawbar

At a glance

Truck and trailer with retractable curtain sides. Often fitted with rear doors. Two or three axles on truck. Two to three axles on trailer

Use

General cargo, often palletised

Description

Although gaining in popularity with UK operators, the drawbar has been a common sight on the Continent for decades. Whether to fit curtainsider or box van bodywork would be an operational decision governed by the balance of load security and access requirements. This German registered example features a close-coupled, twin axle trailer.

The MAN TGA range was launched in 2000 and is notable for its enormous cabs, particularly in the XXL form seen here, a design feature which allows greater engine cooling to meet anticipated emission regulations for many years.

Description

Curtainsider Artic

At a glance
Enclosed load area with retractable fabric curtains. Often fitted with rear doors. Two to three axle tractor unit. One to three axle trailer

Use
Long-distance general cargo, often palletised

The benefits of complete, open-sided loading offered by the curtainsider layout are perfectly illustrated here. The curtainsider is sometimes referred to as a Tautliner, the original name given to the type when developed by the trailer manufacturer, Boalloy.

The Mercedes-Benz Actros 2548 6 x 2 mid-lift tractor unit has the 480 hp version of the company's 12-litre V6 engine and the PowerShift 2 automated gearbox, giving 16 ratios. More powerful versions of the Actros with the 16-litre V8 engine are available with up to 600 hp.

Slide-a-Side Rigid

At a glance
Similar to curtainsider.
Two to four axles

Use
General cargo, often urban multi-drop

Description

The Slide-a-Side is another development of the curtainsider principle, offering more security over a flatbed, and fast operation, making it ideal for the multi-drop role. The bodywork of this example is manufactured by Reeves and suits the nature of this client's business in supplying soft drinks to pubs, clubs, restaurants and shops.

This IVECO Stralis 6 x 2 rigid features a rear-steer third axle, allowing 26-tonne operation with improved manoeuvrability while working in the restrictive urban environments of towns and cities.

Description

Sliding Canopy Drawbar

At a glance

Load platforms completely enclosed by fabric cover. Two or three axle trucks. Two or three axle trailers

Use

Often used for plant and machinery movements

When a platform or flatbed needs covering, the sliding canopy is an excellent method allowing quick and total access to the load. With a fixed bulkhead at the front, the sliding canopy, mounted on up-and-over hoops, can move back and forth on rails set into the side of the load area. This is an ideal solution for machinery movements like this.

This DAF XF105 is a 6 x 2 fitted with the 460 hp version of the MX engine. This combination operates at 44 tonnes and is equipped with a Fassi self-loading arm, with the capacity to lift 1 tonne at a 45-metre reach.

Description

Tilt Articulated Trailer

At a glance
Load area enclosed by drop-side boards with complete fabric cover above. Two or three axle tractor unit. Two or three axle trailer

Use
International general cargo

The tilt has been the favoured trailer for international loads for many decades. Built on a flatbed-type chassis, the tilt has drop boards at the bottom with a removable cover supported by frames with slatted boards in between. The tilt can be stripped, a process known as breaking down, or partially stripped, to access the load. This example has a step-frame chassis to increase load space.

Introduced in 1988, Scania's 143 was the company's top tractor until the introduction of the replacement 4-series trucks. It was equipped with the company's class-leading 14-litre V8 engine.

Description

Skeletal Container Artic

At a glance
Two or three axle tractor unit. Two to three axle trailer

Use
Dedicated trailer for container movement

The standard method for moving containers by road is the skeletal trailer, or skelly.

The skeletal comprises a chassis with outriggers which are fitted with twist locks that correspond with the container's securing sockets. Some skeletals are equipped with a sliding bogie so the trailer can be shortened when carrying a single 20 ft container.

The Mercedes-Benz Actros pictured is a 2546 6 x 2 with a mid-lift axle. The 2546 designation means the tractor unit can handle an imposed load of 25 tonnes and is fitted with a 460 hp engine.

22

Description

Container Drawbar (De-mountable)

At a glance
Two or three axle truck.
Two to three axle trailer

Use
Dedicated container transport

Container drawbar combinations are not that common and this example is somewhat specialised as it also represents a de-mountable system operated by a removal company. In this type of operation it is beneficial to be able to load/unload containers from the vehicle when specialised handling equipment is unavailable, so the containers are fitted with legs which can be raised and lowered. The truck can adjust its height via its air suspension and drive out from underneath a supported container.

This DAF CF85 has a 410 hp version of the 12.9-litre MX engine.

23

Oil Tanker Rigid

At a glance
Tank-type body mounted
on two or three axle
chassis

Use
Short- to medium-range
delivery of heating oil

Description

Although oil tankers come in various sizes, many
will be familiar with the smaller, domestic supply
vehicles such as this. Mounted on chassis of 7.5 to
18 tonnes, these trucks are generally small enough
to access most, beyond the mains, properties. A pto
(power take off) pump from the engine delivers
the fuel through the hose while highly accurate
metering equipment records the amount.

The high glass area of the DAF LF cab range allows
good visibility for manoeuvring in the tight
situations encountered on this type of work.

24

Description

Diesel Tanker Artic

At a glance
Tank body mounted on trailer chassis. Two or three axle tractor unit. One to three axle trailer

Use
Medium- to long-range bulk delivery of diesel fuel

The cylindrical shape of the tanker was developed to help manage the surging properties of a liquid cargo on the move; separate compartments and baffles are included to further reduce this hazardous effect. As it is a free-flowing liquid, petrol can be loaded through the top of the tanker and discharged by gravity from the bottom; other liquids are not so easy and there are a great number of variations to accommodate them.

This Mercedes-Benz Actros 6 x 2 is employed on the delivery of a waste-derived biodiesel product, hence the green livery.

25

Bulk Powder Artic

At a glance

Large tank body often dropping to a point in the centre or at the rear. Two or three axle tractor unit. One to three axle trailer

Use

Medium- to long-range delivery of bulk powders

Description

Bulk powder tankers are used for the movement of a wide range of dry powder goods from agricultural feed to plastic pellets. Because the properties of different products vary, the method of discharge does also. Some trailers will tip on hydraulic rams, while others rely on air pressure or a combination of the two.

The DAF XF 105 pictured is a 6 x 2 unit fitted with a lightweight pusher axle which saves weight over the standard item and frees up valuable chassis space for the discharge pumps and tanks required for emptying the tanker.

26

Vacuum Tanker

At a glance
Heavily reinforced tank body. Two to four axle chassis

Use
Drain clearing, emptying cesspits and slurry tanks

Description

The vacuum tanker (or sludge gulper as it is sometimes unglamorously known) has a vital role in clearing drains to maintain good drainage from our streets and roads. The high-pressure vacuum needed to clear debris requires that the tanker be strongly constructed from steel, with reinforcing bands to prevent the sides from imploding. Loads are disgorged by reversing the pumps or by gravity, with some tanks being raised on hydraulic rams.

This Mercedes-Benz Axor has a 26-tonne GVW and a 6 x 4 chassis layout. The engine is a 7.3-litre unit.

27

Description

Machinery Carrier

At a glance
Open load area that steps down behind the tractor unit. Often has sloping deck after trailer axles

Use
Plant, vehicle and machinery movements

The machinery carrier, sometimes referred to as a semi-low loader, is designed to be easily loaded, with wheeled or tracked vehicles being driven up ramps and over the rear axles along a continuous load area. The load bed is generally planked with wood and chequered plate for grip. These types are often run on air suspension which can be lowered for loading. This tri-axle example easily caters for two tractor units.

The Scania 164 4 x 2 tractor pictured is fitted with a16-litre V8 engine, developing 580 hp, and a Topline cab option with 'Classic' trim.

28

Description

Low Loader

At a glance

Open platform load area with right angle step down behind the tractor unit. Very limited ground clearance. Generally at least three axles on trailer

Use

Heavy plant, vehicle and machinery movements

The low loader trailer utilises a load deck below the height of the trailer wheels to cater for difficult, heavy and awkward loads. An overhead gantry crane is loading this example, but if a heavy tracked or wheeled vehicle were to be carried, the trailer would be split in two. The front part, the swan neck, would remain attached to the tractor unit's fifth wheel, leaving the open bed of the trailer on the ground to accept the load.

This XF105 is tailored to heavy haulage applications, using a sturdy 6 x 4 double drive bogie with hub reduction.

29

Car Transporter Rigid

At a glance
Open load decks which can be raised and lowered. Typically two to three axles

Use
Medium- and long-distance car and van movements

Description

The car transporter is essential for getting new cars to dealerships. The type has evolved a great deal over the years, with the traditional articulated car trailer giving way to a wide range of layouts. This rigid vehicle has capacity for up to six vehicles within its load area, plus a seventh towed on an underlift platform at the rear.

This IVECO Stralis-based transporter is fitted with a steering tag-axle and can operate at a 26-tonne GVW. It is fitted with the Cursor 8 engine, rated at 310 hp, and the Active Time low roof sleeper cab.

30

Bus Transporter Drawbar

At a glance
Open load decks that can be raised and lowered. Tailored to suit commercial vehicle dimensions

Use
Delivery of bus and truck chassis

Description

It is not only new cars that need to be transported. Buses generally leave a manufacturer as a chassis, or even a kit, to be delivered to a coachworks which will then build on the appropriate bodywork. A hydraulically raised upper deck and lower platform form the load area for two buses. When operated with a drawbar trailer a total of three buses, or four trucks, can be carried.

The Volvo FM 26-tonne chassis has bodywork by Lohr of Strasbourg and is fitted with a space saving pusher axle with 17.5-inch wheels.

31

Tipper-truck Rigid

At a glance
Open box body with hinged tailgate. Hydraulic ram mounted under or at the front of the body.

Use
Movement of aggregates and other loose materials

Description

Tipper-trucks, or dump-trucks, are used to deliver loose loads of anything from coal to barley. The principle is generally the same for all types in that a four-sided open box is mounted on the chassis and connected to a hydraulic ram underneath, which raises it to tip the load through a tailgate. Tipping is usually to the rear of the vehicle but some types can tip to the side.

These Volvo FE 4 x 2 tippers have a GVW of 18 tonnes and are fitted with a 6-cylinder 6.2-litre engine, giving 240 hp.

32

Tipper-truck 8 x 4 Rigid

At a glance

Four axle construction chassis with open tipper body. Four steering wheels and four driven wheels

Use

Movement of aggregates and other loose materials

Description

The 8 x 4, or eight-legger tipper, forms the backbone of the UK's construction industry. The type is tough and agile, essential qualities when feeding building projects. All major manufacturers offer special construction versions from their ranges to satisfy this sector, which illustrates its importance. Key features such as sump guards, raised-height cabs, strengthened bumpers, hub reduction and cross differential locks are generally standard.

This Mercedes-Benz Actros 3236 8 x 4 has a GVW of 32 tonnes. The chassis, though very strong, is light enough to allow a full 20-tonne load to be carried.

33

Articulated Tipper (Bulker)

At a glance
High-sided tipper body, often ribbed. Two or three axle tractor unit. Two or three axle trailers

Use
Bulk aggregates, wheat, barley, scrap metal

Description

Articulated tippers, sometimes referred to as bulkers, can operate at up to 44 tonnes GTW on six axles in the UK. The basic design is the same for all types, but construction and materials vary to suit purpose. For the movement of scrap metal, a high-sided design constructed from strong steel with reinforcing ribs is required to contain the load and absorb the punishment of loading.

This Mercedes-Benz Actros 2548 6 x 2 has a pusher axle and a 12-litre V6 engine developing 480 hp. The cab is the high-roof MegaSpace type.

JOHN LAWRIE GROUP
ABERDEEN
www.johnlawrie.com
JOHN LAWRIE GROUP
ABERDEEN
SCOTLAND
SV08 BYA

34

Skip Truck

At a glance
Rigid chassis with two or three axles. Open rear platform with overhead gantry and hydraulic rams

Use
Dedicated vehicle for skip movements

Description

Perhaps the most common of self-loading trucks is the skip truck. Only ever mounted on a rigid chassis, these vehicles are fitted with a lifting gantry connected to hydraulic arms which raise and lower the skip, suspended on chains, over the back of the vehicle. A set of rollers, or feet, are mounted at the rear of the chassis at the lowest point to stop the truck tipping back on the initial lift of a loaded skip.

This Mercedes-Benz Axor 1824 has an 18 tonne-GVW chassis with a 4 x 2 layout and 240 hp.

35

Description

Hook Loader

At a glance
Generally three to four axles. Sometimes operated as a drawbar

Use
Dedicated vehicle for movement of large skips, bottle, paper and clothing banks

The hook loader enables fast self-loading of skips or similar containers. The powerful hydraulic arm hooks under a bracket on the front of the skip and draws it up onto the chassis over rollers. Although often operated as a solo rigid, it is possible to connect a drawbar, in which case the truck can also load the trailer.

This DAF CF85 is an 8 x 4 with 410 hp. The double drive would suit the off-road nature of the vehicle's work. The trailer is a centre axle type with three axles and super single tyres.

36

Glass Carriers

At a glance
Generally two axle rigid chassis. Box type body with angle racking on the outside

Use
Dedicated to movement of large glass panes

Description

The glass carrier is a very specialised vehicle developed to safely deliver a very sensitive cargo. Based on the humble box van, the glass carrier utilises internal racks to secure the panes of glass and is often supplemented, as here, with exterior racks too. The latter are fitted at a 5-degree angle and use movable securing poles to accommodate different size panes.

This IVECO Eurocargo is a 12-tonne, low-height version fitted with the Tector 6-cylinder engine, giving 220 hp. It also has air suspension on the rear axle to protect the load.

37

Furniture (Removal) Van

At a glance
Large rigid vehicle generally with two axles. Box body which often overhangs or incorporates the cab

Use
House removals and furniture delivery

Description

The furniture van, or Pantechnicon as it is sometimes called, is built to the maximum legal dimensions to gain as much load space as possible. Behind the rear wheels, the load platform will sometimes be lower and a large, bottom-hinged door often forms a ramp when lowered. Side access doors are common and numerous lockers lower down provide extra storage.

The DAF CF range evolved from the previous 75 and 85 ranges in 2001. This example has a generously proportioned top sleeper pod to cater for a crew of two or three.

38

Logging Trailer

At a glance

Bare chassis with cross-members and uprights. Generally three axle tractor unit. Two to three axle trailer

Use

Dedicated to log movements

Description

Purpose-built logging trailers are robustly engineered to withstand the rigours of the work they undertake both on- and off-road. A basic skeletal type chassis uses stout cross-members and upright stanchions to secure the logs in transit. While this is very secure, it also affords fast self-loading in the forests which is vital to keep expensive sawmills running.

This Scania 143 is a 6 x 2 tag axle. Tag axles are common on logging trucks as they increase load capacity, guard against axle overloads and can be raised to gain extra grip on the drive axle in tough conditions.

39

Concrete Mixer

At a glance
Three or four axled rigid chassis. Distinctive double-cone rotating drum

Use
Mixing and delivery of concrete

Description

The concrete mixer usually operates in the 26-tonne sector on 3 axles or the 32-tonne sector on 4 axles. The drum must be kept rotating to prevent the load from setting until it reaches its delivery point, at which time the direction is reversed to discharge the concrete. A small auxiliary engine usually provides rotation but some are driven via a pto from the truck's gearbox.

This Volvo FE is a 6 x 4 chassis with 320 hp engine. The Liebherr mixing drum and machinery has a 500-litre water tank to extend the truck's area of operation.

40

Refuse Truck

At a glance
Strong steel body mounted on two or three axle rigid chassis. Lifting mechanism for bins at rear

Use
Rubbish and recycled waste collection

Description

The refuse truck has evolved over the years into a highly specialised machine capable of processing different types of recyclable material. Usually operated by local authorities, many different styles are produced depending on the recycling capabilities of a given county. Generally, all have a strong steel body with reinforcing ribs and hydraulic rams inside for compressing and disgorging the material.

This Mercedes-Benz Econic chassis is powered by natural gas. The Econic range is ideally suited for urban and municipal roles, with a low-height cab for ease of access and a large glass area for all-round vision

41

Rigid Horsebox

At a glance
Two or three axle rigid chassis. Flush-sided body. Loading to rear or sides

Use
Movement of horses

Description

Over the past two decades or so, the traditional and somewhat spartan horsebox has evolved into a state-of-the-art machine, based on mid- to top-range chassis from the leading manufacturers. Examples like this can accommodate multiple horses along with all their kit, and provides rest and recreational facilities for crews.

The new Volvo FH range was introduced in 2008 and features a 13-litre engine with outputs from 400 to 520 hp. This 26-tonne example has 440 hp and is fitted with Volvo's I-Shift automatic gearbox. The 6 x 2 chassis features a rear steer back axle and all-round air suspension.

42

Description

Road/Rail Trucks

At a glance
Truck chassis mounted with additional rail wheels front and back

Use
Maintenance and repair of rail infrastructure

The railway system is dependent on trucks for its maintenance. With many stretches of track being inaccessible to ordinary vehicles, specialised trucks and plant have been developed to suit the purpose. These vehicles carry a set of train wheels at the front and back of the chassis which can be lowered into the rails allowing the vehicle to drive, via its road wheels, along the track.

This road/rail example is built on a Volvo FM 6 x 4 chassis and pulls a purpose-built trailer-mounted piece of plant which can also travel on the tracks.

43

Heavy Haulage STGO Categories

At a glance
Multi-axle truck and low-loader trailer combinations

Use
Abnormal indivisible loads

Description

In the UK any load over the usual 44-tonne maximum comes under STGO (Special Types General Order) regulations. There are three bands, STGO 1 covers loads up to 50 tonnes, STGO 2 up to 80 tonnes and STGO 3 up to 150 tonnes. Tractor units often have four or more axles and may be ballasted, in which case they tow the trailer from a heavy-duty hitch rather than a fifth-wheel coupling. Trailers can have many axles and are sometimes modular with axle and load area sections that can be added as needed.

This Volvo FH16 is an 8 x 4 chassis fitted with super-single wheels on the two front axles. It has a 16-litre, 6-cylinder engine, giving 660 hp.

44

Recovery Truck

At a glance
Rigid chassis. Two to four axles. Hydraulic lifting boom

Use
Heavy vehicle recovery

Description

When trucks break down or have an accident they require another truck to recover them. Often referred to as a wrecker, the modern recovery truck owes its ancestry to the conversion of ex-military vehicles following the First World War. Early vehicles made do with simple lifting booms and winches, but today's examples are somewhat more cutting edge. Powerful hydraulic underlifts, mounted at the rear of the vehicle, are now the most common type in use and fully freighted 44-tonne artics can be towed.

This IVECO Trakker 8 x 4 is fitted with Brimec lifting gear and two 35,000 kg winches.

Truck Talk

Some industry words explained

AdBlue:	Additive injected into the exhaust to lower emissions
Artic:	Abbreviation for an articulated vehicle
Bogie:	Two or more axles mounted together
Differential Locks (Diff locks):	locks which drive wheels together for better traction
Fifth wheel:	Device fitted to tractor units for coupling to trailers
GVW:	Gross Vehicle Weight, the maximum permitted operating weight for a solo vehicle
GTW:	Gross Train Weight, the maximum permitted operating weight for truck and trailer combinations
hp:	Horsepower. Accepted measurement of engine output
Pallet:	Wooden frame with slatted top for stacking goods; can be picked up by a forklift truck
Rigid:	Single chassis vehicle without articulation
Tractor Unit:	Powered part of an articulated combination. Sometimes referred to as just the tractor, just the unit or sometimes cab or cab unit.

International system for classifying commercial vehicle wheel and drive layouts

When spoken, the 'x' symbol is pronounced as 'by', i.e. 4 x 2 is 4 by 2.

The first part refers to the total number of wheels; the second part refers to the number of wheels that are driven. NB. Double wheels on one axle are counted as one wheel.

Steering axle   Drive axle   Plain axle

Some typical examples

4 x 2	6 x 2 (pusher)	6 x 2 (tag)	6 x 4	8 x 4

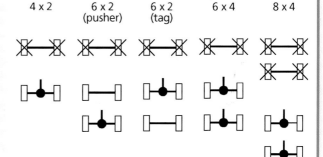

Anatomy of a Truck

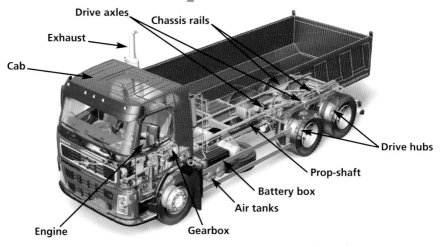

Drive axles

Chassis rails

Exhaust

Cab

Drive hubs

Prop-shaft

Battery box

Air tanks

Engine

Gearbox